Original title:
Bananas and Daydreams

Copyright © 2025 Creative Arts Management OÜ
All rights reserved.

Author: Zachary Prescott
ISBN HARDBACK: 978-1-80586-419-6
ISBN PAPERBACK: 978-1-80586-891-0

Tasting Sunshine

A fruit so bright, it slips my hand,
I chase it down across the sand.
With every bite, a giggle flows,
It's silly how this laughter grows.

In every peel, a zany twist,
An unexpected turn, I can't resist.
With yellow smiles that fill the air,
I dance around without a care.

Golden Reveries

In dreams of gold, I feel so light,
Jumping high, oh what a sight!
The little fruit that leads the way,
Turns shadows into bright ballet.

With every munch, a silly cheer,
Imaginary friends draw near.
We frolic in a world so grand,
With laughter echoing through the land.

Grove of Unfurling Thoughts

A grove where giggles grow on trees,
Each swing and sway brings jitters, whee!
Thoughts unfurl like petals, bright,
Amidst the fun and pure delight.

A gathering of quirks so sweet,
As silly stories dance on feet.
With laughter ringing through the leaves,
A joyful heart, the mind achieves!

Escaping into the Golden

I take a trip, a zany ride,
Into the golden, joy my guide.
Each twist and turn, a playful tease,
Tickles my soul, puts me at ease.

The laughter sparkles in the sun,
A chase with fruit, so much fun!
I tumble down this silly lane,
A jester lost, yet full of gain.

Daylit Delights

In a world where smiles are fried,
And giggles float like clouds of cream,
Laughter bounces down the slide,
With joy, we sail on a silly dream.

Sunshine spills like lemonade,
Tickling toes with golden light,
Bouncing balls in a grand parade,
Where every moment feels just right.

Palette of Whimsy

Colors splash on the canvas bright,
With splatters of giggle and swirl,
A splash of charm in morning light,
　As silly thoughts begin to twirl.

Paintbrush dances, oh, how it funs,
It tickles the heart and skips the beat,
Each stroke whispers of made-up puns,
Creating laughter that feels so sweet.

Peeling Layers of Thought

In the kitchen, thoughts unpeel,
Like sweet surprises in each layer,
Funny faces start to squeal,
As pondering leads to playful flair.

A slip of whimsy, a dash of cream,
Ideas tumble in a wobbly stack,
Bizarre and bright, they reign supreme,
In this merry world, there's no lack.

The Dance of Fantasy

Feet shuffle in the air so free,
As giggles pirouette round the room,
Twinkling tales like leaves from a tree,
Spinning joy, dispelling gloom.

Each squeaky toy plays a funny tune,
With a hop, skip, and a wink, we glide,
Under the golden afternoon,
In a world where glee cannot hide.

A Serenade in Sunshine

In the shade of leafy trees,
A monkey swings, oh what a tease!
With a grin that's wide and bright,
He juggles fruit from left to right.

Laughter echoes, fills the air,
As squirrels join the playful bear.
They dance and prance without a care,
In a world that's light and rare.

A picnic feast on checkered cloth,
With slips and trips, the laughter swath.
Oh, how delights may sometimes slip,
While we all take a silly trip.

So raise a glass, let's toast the fun,
To silly tales 'neath the bright sun.
With fruity treats, we take our stand,
In this whimsical, goofy land.

Tales of Golden Delights

Once upon a time with cheer,
In a land where smiles appear.
Golden treasures roll around,
Creating giggles, funny sounds.

A jester with a crown of fruit,
Danced along in silly boots.
He tripped and tumbled on the ground,
Yet laughter was the only sound.

Chased by geese with wiggly feet,
They formed a line, a funny fleet.
In every chase, a slip and slide,
With silly grins they took in stride.

So gather 'round, for tales untold,
Of giggles shared and joys of old.
In this land of endless mirth,
We find pure joy, and endless worth.

Wandering Between the Trees

In a grove where laughter grows,
Chasing shadows, no one knows,
A monkey sways with silly glee,
While squirrels plot a jester's spree.

A picnic spread with fruity flair,
Sticky fingers, no time to care,
Birds serenade, a comical tune,
Underneath the lazy noon.

The breeze weaves tales both bright and bold,
While tales of mischief quickly unfold,
Twirling around, so carefree and spry,
With giggles floating up to the sky.

Drowsy Daylight

Beneath the sun, where dreams conspire,
A snoozing cat, her world's a choir,
Pillow forts and noodle fights,
Pajama days and candy bites.

Clouds like puffs, so soft and white,
Float past a kite, oh such a sight,
Ice cream drips down silly chins,
While laughter dances, spun like spins.

A jolly breeze whispers in play,
Time takes a nap, happy and wavy,
Sunbeams twist like ribbons of gold,
In this slumber, life feels bold.

Light Play in a Sunny Realm

Colors swirl in a playful ballet,
A romp through fields where giggles sway,
Butterflies bounce in the morning light,
Sparkling grass where whispers ignite.

Jumping in puddles, splashes abound,
With laughter, our joy is profound,
A woeful frog leaps with a splash,
While the sun smiles, and shadows dash.

Frolicking fairies croon a bright rhyme,
As we lose track of the passing time,
In a sunny realm where the heart may leap,
And fun is a treasure we gladly keep.

Melodies of a Golden Aura

In a world that frolics with sound,
Happiness bounces all around,
A curious duck with a quack-quack tune,
Invents a song that makes us swoon.

With giggles blooming like daisies fair,
Chasing wind, we dance in the air,
Balloons float high with joy and cheer,
While silly hats make everything clear.

The sun dips low, painting skies aglow,
Every step resonates in a playful flow,
Crickets join in the grand delight,
As twilight wraps the day in light.

Sun-Drenched Reflections

In the sunlit park, a silly thought,
A yellow peel where laughter's caught.
Chasing shadows, we run with glee,
Around the trees, just you and me.

Giggles burst like bubbles high,
While playful monkeys swing and fly.
A twist of fate in every jest,
On this bright day, we are the best.

Fragrant Whirls of Fancy

A silly scent wafts through the air,
Wiggle-wobbles without a care.
Imagining worlds where we can dance,
In swooping arcs of sweet romance.

With every spin, there's laughter loud,
The talking fruits draw in a crowd.
A swirl of colors, they all parade,
In this sweet show, we won't evade.

Harvesting Light

Under the glow of a summer sun,
We jot down jokes, it's all in fun.
Each silly pun, a wink and cheer,
Pulling smiles from those far and near.

Gathering rays like they're ripe and bold,
With every chuckle, new tales unfold.
In this bright harvest, we share the light,
Creating laughter from morning to night.

Dreaming with a Hint of Sweetness

Pillows of cream, our heads in the clouds,
Crafting wild tales, too funny to shroud.
With sleepy grins, we spin around,
In this sweet scheme, where joy is found.

A sprinkle of whimsy, a dash of fun,
The world's a stage, we're on the run.
In every giggle, dreams take flight,
Bringing sunshine to the cozy night.

A Carousel of Sunlit Delights

Round and round the laughter spins,
Chasing shadows, where the fun begins.
A ride on whimsy, bright and fast,
Joyful moments, forever cast.

Radiant colors paint the air,
Giggles echo everywhere.
In the breeze, we find our chase,
With a wink and silly face.

Carousels with chattering glee,
Twisting tales of jubilee.
Hands held tight against the spins,
Where the silly never ends.

Onward we swirl, a merry throng,
To the beat of a playful song.
Smiles painted, hearts so free,
In the light, just you and me.

Meringue Clouds and Citrus Smiles

Puffy dreams on fluffy skies,
Sipping joy from sweet surprise.
A zesty twist in every bite,
Fruity giggles, pure delight.

Whipped up wonders float above,
Sour snickers, tastes we love.
Bubbles tickle, laughter gleams,
Meringue magic, swirling dreams.

Citron hues and lemon beams,
Curled up dreams like candy streams.
As we dance through fluffy air,
Life's a feast, without a care.

In a world of candied cheer,
Every moment brings us near.
With a grin, we take a chance,
On meringue clouds, we waltz and prance.

Swaying to the Rhythm of Nature

Dancing leaves in playful sway,
Nature hums a bright ballet.
Each breeze whispers, soft and light,
Under stars, our dreams take flight.

To the tunes of chirping birds,
We sing along without words.
Bouncing flowers, tapping feet,
Life's a jig, so wild and sweet.

With the rustle of green delight,
We twirl beneath the moonlit night.
Gentle rhythms, flowing free,
A nature's waltz, just you and me.

Stars like sprinkles in the sky,
We sway and dance, oh my, oh my!
Every moment, laughter's friend,
A symphony that'll never end.

Harvest of Joyful Reveries

Baskets full of giggles bright,
Laughter echoes, morning light.
With every pick, a chuckle grows,
In this patch of playful prose.

Silly stories in the fields,
Nature's bounty, joy it yields.
Frolicking toes in earthy ground,
Finding glee where fun is found.

Wandering through the sunlit maze,
Harvesting smiles in endless ways.
Every fruit is filled with cheer,
A silly grin, a hearty cheer.

Underneath this joyous sun,
Days of laughter, boundless fun.
With each treasure, joy we share,
In a fest of whimsy, love's laid bare.

Golden Slips of Imagination

A yellow twist in morning light,
Bright smiles tangle, take to flight.
Floating thoughts like playful breeze,
Slipping into jokes with ease.

In every bite, a laugh unfolds,
Whispers of tales both fresh and bold.
Chasing shadows with silly glee,
Tickling notions that set us free.

Riding peaks of laughter high,
As giggles dance and swirl nearby.
Warming hearts with fruity fun,
Beneath the glow of the morning sun.

So come and join this merry spree,
With golden slips and wild esprit.
In this realm of silly games,
We find the joy in all our names.

The Cocktail of Curiosity

A twist of fruit in lovely glass,
Sipping thoughts as breezes pass.
Curious sips of laughter sweet,
Mixing dreams with every treat.

A splash of whimsy, dash of cheer,
Creating moments we hold dear.
Stirred with kindness, shaken bright,
Sparkling giggles in the night.

Garnished with a wacky grin,
Each sip brings out the child within.
Unexpected flavors whirl and blend,
Crafting joy that will not end.

So raise a toast to silly hearts,
In this cocktail, laughter starts.
With every drop of joy we taste,
A wondrous life, we will not waste.

Serene Escapades

Whimsical trails where laughter roams,
Beyond the hills, where nothing's combs.
Flying kites with pants askew,
Chasing clouds of golden hue.

Skip and hop through vibrant fields,
Silly dreams, the heart it yields.
Finding joy in every nook,
Where time feels like a playful book.

Frolicking under the bright sun's glow,
Imaginary worlds begin to grow.
Bouncing off the silly side,
In this realm, we take our ride.

Come join this quest, so bright and clear,
Where smiles and giggles draw us near.
Together we will wander far,
Chasing wonders like a shooting star.

Midnight Musings in Dappled Light

Under the moon, where silliness blooms,
Whispers of joy fill the rooms.
Dappled shadows dance and play,
In the night where dreams sway.

Nonsense tales take flight with grace,
As laughter paints the starry space.
With every chuckle, wisdom shared,
In moonlit moments, no one cared.

Giggling sprites on twilight's wing,
Baffle the world with the joy they bring.
Twirling thoughts in soft moon's glow,
Through laughter, we'll learn what we don't know.

So let your mind freely roam,
In the night, feel right at home.
For in this light, we find delight,
Endless giggles shine so bright.

Festive Whirls in Pajama Land

In pajamas bright, we twirl around,
Slippers sliding, laughter's sound.
Teddy bears come join the spree,
In this wild, zany jubilee.

Cupcakes frolic, gleaming plate,
Dance with socks, oh silly fate.
Syrupy giggles fill the air,
As we twirl without a care.

Surprise! A blanket fort appears,
Our kingdom of fluff, let's cheer and jeer.
Popcorn storms and comic tales,
In this realm where craziness sails.

Here in the land of dreamy play,
Socks and snacks, hooray hooray!
Cup of cocoa, froths that swirl,
In pajama land, let's laugh and whirl.

Chasing Magic in the Orchard

In orchards bright, we skip and weave,
With treasures sweet, you won't believe!
The sky wears shades of silly blue,
As we embark on quests anew.

Squirrels play the jester's part,
With acorn hats, they steal our heart.
We pick the fruit with giddy cheer,
A feast of joy is drawing near!

Side-stepping bees that dance around,
While we twirp and leap, earthbound.
Chasing shadows, laughter's sound,
Every corner, magic found.

Under trees where secrets roam,
We drink the nectar, calling it home.
With giggles echoing every day,
Our orchard's mischief leads the way.

Hues of Bliss beneath a Golden Canopy

Under a canopy, golden light,
Colors dance, oh what a sight!
Painted skies with splashes bright,
Our joyful hearts take joyful flight.

We flutter like leaves in joyful glee,
Each moment wrapped in mystery.
Pineapple hats, so bizarre and grand,
Chasing colors in this wonderland.

With giggles spilling like the sun,
Every prank is just good fun.
In this world of laughter's bloom,
We conjure dreams that fill the room.

As colors bleed through leafy trails,
We ride the breeze, we tell our tales.
In hues of bliss, we laugh and find,
A tapestry of joy, intertwined.

Lush Landscapes of Unexpected Joy

In lush patches of grass so deep,
We invent wonders, loud and cheap.
With giggles bound, we climb and race,
Turning every frown to a sunny face.

Unexpected sprinkles, sudden rains,
We splash and dance, forget our pains.
With puddle jumps and silly shouts,
Our laughter echoes, there's no doubts.

Butterflies wearing silly hats,
Join our frolic, imagine that!
Wiggly worms become our pals,
Singing songs of whimsical gales.

Through landscapes dreamy, wild and free,
We catch the sun, a jubilant spree.
With every twist and silly ploy,
We gather moments of pure joy.

Lullabies of Lush Landscapes

In pajamas, I take flight,
Through jungles blooming bright.
Lizards dance on leafy trails,
While I giggle at their tales.

Dreams wear hats made from green leaves,
Fluttering like swaying cleaves.
Tropical fruits with silly grins,
In my head, the fun begins.

Sunshine tickles all around,
Whispers echo, silly sound.
Pineapple brings its pals, it seems,
Entering my slide of dreams.

Giggling streams of flowing cheer,
Nature's humor always near.
I'll frolic through this merry scene,
Chasing clouds that smile and preen.

Radiant Silhouettes

Shadows play on summer grass,
As laughter flows, the moments pass.
Silhouettes of cheeky sprites,
Dancing under shimmering lights.

Chasing options, wild and free,
Sliding down a gnarled tree.
Orange peels and daisy crowns,
Fashion moments, giggles drown.

Whimsical creatures peek and tease,
Tickling fancies like a breeze.
With each twist and turn about,
I twirl with joy, there's no doubt.

Silly shapes in colors bright,
Paint my heart with pure delight.
Above, the sky joins in the fun,
Frolicking 'neath the radiant sun.

Sweet Cloudscapes

Fluffy wonders drifting high,
Marshmallow shapes in a cotton sky.
Mischief mingles with the air,
Teasing dreams without a care.

Laughter sprinkles like warm rain,
Jokes unfold, a gentle gain.
In these sweet, imagined lands,
Giggles burst like soft rubber bands.

Tickled cheeks by drifting fluff,
Every moment feels just enough.
With each soft and fluffy grind,
Whimsical thoughts are intertwined.

Carousels of dreams unfold,
With stories waiting to be told.
Up above, the colors burst,
Painting joy, quenching thirst.

Beneath the Canopy of Thought

Underneath a leafy dome,
Silly creatures call this home.
Wiggly vines and giggling bugs,
Gather round for hugs and shrugs.

Sipping nectar sweet and bright,
Wishing for a plastic flight.
Tangled stories twist and spin,
As chirps and chuckles now begin.

Pineapple hats on sprites' small heads,
Napping softly in their beds.
Waking writes of nighttime dreams,
Full of laughter, silly schemes.

Clouds of foam and shades of green,
The funniest sights I've ever seen.
Beneath this canopy so grand,
Wanderers giggle, hand in hand.

Fantasies in Golden Hues

In a kitchen bright and bold,
Yellow fruits are tales untold.
Juggling one with pure delight,
Silly faces, what a sight!

Peels dance in a whirlwind spree,
Chasing laughter, wild and free.
With every slip, a giggle grows,
Fragrant dreams, where humor flows.

A monkey hops, a curious gaze,
In this world of fruity plays.
Chasing shadows, light and spry,
With each twist, we reach the sky.

So grab a bunch, let's have some fun,
Life's a game, we've just begun.
In sunshine bright, we'll giggle loud,
In our golden haze, we're oh so proud.

Languid Kinship

Underneath the leafy shade,
Silly thoughts begin to wade.
A cousin who can also peel,
Laughing at a mazy wheel.

Swaying gently in the breeze,
Dancing like the clumsy bees.
With each twirl, we stumble, glide,
In this shared, amusing ride.

Lighthearted whispers through the air,
Funny faces, all kinds of flair.
Joy resides where smiles unfold,
In the warmth of stories told.

As the sun dips down, we cheer,
In this bond that we hold dear.
A legacy of laughter spun,
Sweetened tales, we've just begun.

Ethereal Sunshine

In a world of pretend delight,
Glowing fruit, oh what a sight!
Chasing rainbows, skies so blue,
In this realm, we'll start anew.

With a giggle and a run,
We'll poke at shadows, just for fun.
A world where silly reigns supreme,
Floating high on a vivid dream.

Sprinkling laughter like confetti,
Jumbled words, our heads all ready.
Each thought a bubble, light as air,
Life is strange, we haven't a care.

So let the sunshine lift us high,
In this whimsical, endless sky.
With zest alive, we skip and prance,
Savoring this absurd romance.

Sun-kissed Delirium

When the golden rays arrive,
Colorful creatures come alive.
With every twist, a spark ignites,
Silliness in joyful hikes.

Fragrant wafts of playful cheer,
Chasing echoes far and near.
Wobbling laughter, cries of glee,
In this zesty jubilee.

Carefree spirits, light as air,
Creating memories everywhere.
In our madcap golden hue,
Adventures call, there's much to do!

Sunset paints the scene so bright,
As we dance into the night.
With hearts so full, we can't resist,
This life we share, a sweet twist.

Lush Visions of Portfolios

In a jungle of thoughts, ideas sprout,
Bright yellow dreams, twist and shout.
With laughter they swing from tree to tree,
Chasing the sun, light as can be.

Ideas jump high, like frogs in delight,
Crafting visions that take to flight.
Each giggle a splash, a paint of glee,
Building a world of pure jubilee.

A portfolio full of a smile's grant,
With silly antics, like a playful chant.
Dancing around like monkeys on a beam,
In a merry-go-round of a whimsical dream.

Tropical sketches swirl and sway,
Cartwheeling thoughts come out to play.
In this canvas where laughter spins,
The lush visions start as the fun begins.

The Essence of Blissful Drift

Floating on clouds, soft as a sigh,
Whimsical thoughts, the mind can fly.
Tickling the breeze with a giggle or two,
A blissful escape, just me and you.

Colors collide in a playful spree,
Where every thought tastes like candy, you see.
Wandering through realms of laughter and cheer,
In a silly frolic, all worries disappear.

Jellybean dreams dance on the air,
As we glide on a whim, without a care.
Hopping from one thought to another,
Finding joy in the space to discover.

The essence of drift is sweet and light,
A carnival twirl, a joyful flight.
With each gentle wave, a chuckle is found,
In the land of the silly, where bliss does abound.

Vivid Threads of Whimsy

In a tapestry bright, where fun intertwines,
Gathering laughter like ripe, juicy vines.
Threads of delight in patterns so bold,
Spinning tales of giggles, never old.

Each stitch a smile, each knot a cheer,
Weaving the moments, so precious, so dear.
Unruly colors mix and play,
In the land of mischief, where we sway.

The fabric of fun wraps us, so snug,
With sunshine and whimsy in every hug.
A patchwork of giggles under the sun,
In this crazy quilt, we come together as one.

Vivid and bright, these threads we sew,
Creating a realm where the good vibes flow.
With joyful echoes, we sing and shout,
In the world of whimsy, there's never a doubt.

A Dappled Odyssey

Embark on a journey through giggle and glee,
On waves of laughter, come sail with me.
Where shadows dance in the warmth of the sun,
A dappled adventure has just begun.

Sipping on sunshine, life's zesty fair,
With silly companions, we haven't a care.
Chasing the whispers of wonder and light,
In our frolicsome travel, spirits take flight.

With each little hop over puddles of cheer,
In this playful quest, joy is so near.
Twirling through moments both bright and absurd,
Finding delight in each silly word.

So onward we roam, with smiles on display,
In landscapes of laughter, come join the play.
A journey of whimsy, a treasure to hold,
In this dappled odyssey, let joy unfold.

Sweetly Unraveled

In a land of curved delights,
Where peels slip and giggles bloom,
A fruit parade takes silly flights,
Chasing laughter in the room.

Jesters in yellow suits skipped,
Tripping over laughter pools,
A frolic where joy is tipped,
And everyone plays the fool.

With every munch, a round of cheer,
Silly faces come alive,
In every bite, there's nothing near,
A twist on how we thrive.

So let the sun shine ever bright,
In this circus of delight,
Sweets like whispers in the night,
Unraveling our hearts in flight.

A Canvas of Cheerful Shadows

Under skies of rainbow hue,
Where giggles dance on dotted lines,
Curved treasures sprout anew,
Painting tales with silly signs.

Puppets made of fruity dreams,
Swing from branches, full of cheer,
Their laughter bursting at the seams,
Tickling the clouds up high, so near.

With splotches of orange and green,
The art of joy forever flows,
A canvas with no in-between,
Where every smile brightly glows.

So gather 'round, let colors mix,
In a whirl of content moods,
Creating laughter's perfect tricks,
With fruity fun in cheerful woods.

Swaying with Gentle Fantasies

In a meadow where heehaws sing,
And shadows sway with light and breeze,
A twist of joy on a tiny swing,
Tickling toes through grassy seas.

Little critters leap and bound,
Chasing dreams so vivid bright,
Where the giggle-glow is found,
In a garden filled with light.

With every twirl, a silliness,
Unfurls like petals in the sun,
Creating moments full of bliss,
As laughter weaves, and dreams run.

So take a ride on whimsy's train,
And let your spirit float so free,
In the joy, there's no more pain,
Just playful thoughts and jests of glee.

Daylight Reveries

In the glow of bright delight,
Curves of fun twist in the air,
A break from shadows, in full sight,
Where giggles spark a funny flare.

Silly whispers weave through trees,
With every turn, a chuckle grows,
As time drips down like honey bees,
Dancing 'round in cheerful flows.

When the world spins topsy-turvy,
And colors swirl in vivid schemes,
We chase the sun, not feeling surly,
Caught up in light, we weave our dreams.

So let the daylight guide our play,
With laughter ringing like a bell,
In the whimsy of every day,
Each golden moment casts a spell.

Serene Slopes of Delight

In the garden where laughter grows,
Silly monkeys strike funny poses,
Wobbling on their playful feet,
Chasing ants and feeling neat.

Clouds tumble like fluffy sheep,
While the sun giggles and peeks,
Magic twirls in the afternoon,
Tickling toes as we swoon.

Giggling flowers dance in rows,
Winds whispering silly prose,
Sipping tea with a cheeky grin,
Life's a game, come jump in!

Rainbows paint the sky so bold,
Stories of laughter yet untold,
We'll play in this land of glee,
Forever young, wild, and free.

Fool's Paradise on a Silk Road

On a path of shimmering gold,
A jester's laugh, a tale retold,
Lemons leap into the air,
Bouncing clouds without a care.

Tango with a jiggly sprite,
Under the stars shining bright,
Snack on giggles, chew on dreams,
Life is nothing but silly schemes.

Kites fly high, ribbons untamed,
While jolly tunes are softly named,
A teapot sings a wacky song,
In this world, we all belong.

Sipping joy from sugar cups,
Hiccups burst with silly ups,
Every twist a chuckle's cue,
In this tale, it's me and you.

The Fruit of Fantasy's Embrace

In a land where giggles bloom,
A playful breeze dispels the gloom,
Jellybeans rain from the trees,
Sour patches dance in the breeze.

Ticklish vines twirl with glee,
Hopping over a giggly bee,
Colors splash like paint on walls,
In this world where nonsense calls.

Peaches smile with sugary delight,
While gnomes play hopscotch at night,
Laughter's fruit, sweet as can be,
Sharing joy so endlessly.

While the moon spins a wacky tale,
All our dreams set sail,
In this wonder, let us race,
With laughter wrapping in embrace.

Chasing Shadows and Citrus Hues

In a garden of shadows that play,
Sunbeams slip and sway,
Lively limes, in a whirl,
Dance together in a twirl.

Wobbling on the grassy floor,
We tickle clouds, they ask for more,
Chasing whispers of fruity cheer,
While the sunset holds us near.

Silly shadows hide and seek,
Underneath the fruit-tree peak,
Slicing laughter with a grin,
In this place, adventures begin.

We toss the world, oh what a ride!
In citrus dreams, we glide,
Tickled pink, we pirouette,
Leaving behind a happy debt.

Pondering in the Afternoon Sun

In bright yellow peels, they lie,
Curved like a smile, oh my, oh my.
I ponder their sweetness, a snack divine,
While sunbeams dance with a cheeky twine.

A monkey swings with a playful grin,
Chasing shadows, where laughter begins.
As juice drips down, I can't help but laugh,
Is this adventure or just a sweet gaffe?

The leaves rustle secrets, they whisper to me,
In this silly hour, I'm wild and free.
Each bite a giggle, each sip a cheer,
In this golden world, nothing to fear.

So here's to the fruit that brightens my day,
In whimsical musings, I'll forever stay.
With sunlight above, and joy all around,
In this goofy realm, bliss can be found.

Sweet Enchantment

A fruit basket filled with glee,
Winks at me from the kitchen spree.
Each shiny curve, a playful tease,
Whispers of laughter in a zephyr breeze.

With a sprinkle of sugar and a dash of fun,
Every nibble sparks joy, a race to outrun.
Like giggling children on a sunny spree,
This fruity delight invites jubilee.

The blender hums a ridiculous tune,
As smoothies swirl and glimmer like a moon.
Sticky fingers and silly grins, oh my,
In the realm of sweetness, who could deny?

So come let's frolic, delight in the taste,
Of mischief and magic, no moment to waste.
In every munch and every sip shared,
Laughter and cheer are freshly prepared.

Tropical Daydreaming

Under palm trees, I start to sway,
With visions of treasures that dance and play.
Each flavor bursts like confetti bright,
In my sunny world, everything feels right.

A tropical vision with comical flair,
Bright colors splash like paint in the air.
Lemonade rivers and jellybean hills,
Every sip brings giggles and silly thrills.

In this carnival of fruity delight,
Joy bubbles over, taking flight.
With a twirl and a whirl, I can't help but be,
Lost in this land filled with jubilee.

So let's frolic beneath the bright sun,
With a basket of joy for everyone.
In laughter's embrace, we'll always remain,
In this whimsical land, joy is our gain.

Lemonade Skies

Beneath the sky of zesty hue,
I sip on sunshine, yes it's true.
The clouds are giggling, their shapes like treats,
A carnival of flavors in soft breezy beats.

With sips of joy and twinkling eyes,
I imagine worlds where wonder never dies.
Each gulp a journey, a whimsical ride,
Where silly dreams play, bubbling with pride.

As horses of jelly slide down rainbows,
And laughter erupts wherever it flows.
In this paradise painted with delight,
Even the stars seem funnier at night.

So gather your merriment and dance along,
In lemonade skies, we all belong.
With a wink and a grin, let's toast to the cheer,
In this fruity fiesta, love knows no fear.

Tropical Escape on a Cloud

Drifting high on a fluffy smile,
Riding waves of laughter for a while.
The sun winks down, a cheeky friend,
With every giggle, the troubles end.

Juicy thoughts float in the air,
Tickling my mind without a care.
A paradise where silliness reigns,
Chasing shadows, we dance in chains.

Bright colors swirl in cotton dreams,
Waving 'hello' from ice cream streams.
Bouncing bubbles, all shapes and sizes,
Each one pops with surprising prizes.

In this whimsy, we jive and play,
Turning moments to sun-kissed clay.
Silly hats tiptoe on our heads,
As we leap through life in playful threads.

Whispers of Happiness in the Breeze

A giggle drifts on the warm, light air,
Spreading joy like confetti everywhere.
The trees sway, laughing along,
With silly songs that can't go wrong.

Clouds gather round, curious to hear,
The whispered secrets that tickle the ear.
A breeze dances, twirling at play,
Singing tales of a vibrant day.

Butterflies join in the fun tonight,
Winging past with a flurry of light.
They flutter about in a colorful race,
Painting the world with a giggling grace.

As shadows stretch and twinkle above,
We spread our arms, feeling the love.
Each breath we take, a bubbling cheer,
With every heartbeat, the magic's near.

Melodies of Joy among the Leaves

Under the canopy where the giggles play,
Leaves rustle softly, inviting the sway.
Laughter sprouts from the roots below,
Sprinkling happiness with every flow.

Squirrels dance in their tiny suits,
While birds sing silly, playful hoots.
Each note bounces through the green and gold,
Tales of frolic joyously unfold.

A carpet of petals cushions our feet,
As whimsical creatures spin to the beat.
The music of nature blends in a swirl,
Inviting us all to dance and twirl.

With every rustle, there's a spark so bright,
Chasing shadows with pure delight.
We leap in tune, our spirits set free,
In this joyful realm, we find our glee.

The Sweetness of a Sunlit Dream

Beneath the sun's cheerful embrace,
Imagination blooms in a joyful place.
Sugary whispers float through the air,
Crafting laughter from the warm, soft glare.

Each moment is a flickering flame,
With bright ideas calling our name.
We share our smiles with the vibrant skies,
As silly thoughts dance with playful sighs.

Lemonade rivers flowing with cheer,
Turning our frowns into bright grins here.
Sweet treats tumble from the palm of bliss,
Inviting a giggle, who could resist?

In the warmth of dreams, we twine and spin,
Where every adventure is ready to begin.
With every chuckle, the world feels right,
A sunlit joy that sparkles so bright.

Echoes of Vibrant Whispers

In a realm where laughter blooms,
The fruit brigade dances in costumes.
Umbrellas twirl beneath the sun,
Joyful giggles have just begun.

A wiggle here, a wiggle there,
Fruitful antics fill the air.
With every peel, a chuckle spills,
Chasing shadows, chasing thrills.

Pineapples wear hats made of cheese,
Lemons juggling with effortless ease.
In this world, silliness reigns,
Tickling hearts like gentle rains.

Each banter sweet, each jest a treat,
Life is ripe, adventurous, neat.
Parties erupt on every street,
With fruity friends, life's a feast!

A Tapestry of Sunlit Thoughts

Swaying gently on the breeze,
Thoughts like fruit hang from the trees.
With every brush of sunlight's kiss,
A world spins round in silly bliss.

Coconuts chatter, teasing the breeze,
Limes in shades of vibrant tease.
Ideas pop like fizzy drinks,
Bubbles rise as laughter winks.

Fluttering leaves, whispers of fun,
Daring dreams under the sun.
In this canvas, colors collide,
Joy is endless, like a wild ride.

Pineapples grin, with crowns held high,
Melons giggle as they pass by.
A world woven from laughter's thread,
In this tapestry, no dread.

Dreams from a Distant Grove

In a grove where giggles grow,
Wacky fruits put on a show.
Dreams take flight on branches tall,
Silliness beckons, come one, come all.

Peering through leaves of lime and peach,
Every bonkers tale, within reach.
Whispers of joy danced in the air,
Fruits and fables, beyond compare.

Ripe thoughts plucked from high above,
Softest hints of playful love.
Nature's circus, full of charm,
Wrapping the world in a fruity warm.

We twirl amongst all shades of glee,
Finding magic in every spree.
Tomorrow's laughter waits to bloom,
In a grove of dreams, there's always room.

Curving Conversations

Beneath the trees, voices curve,
Funny tales that all preserve.
Fruitful exchanges, sweet and bright,
Banter that dances in warm light.

Cheeky cherries share their schemes,
As oranges float on sunny beams.
Every pun a juicy delight,
Sprinkling giggles left and right.

Twisting words, a playful game,
In this garden, fun's the name.
Tangerines sing, lemons tease,
The air is filled with light hearted ease.

So come and join, grab a seat,
In this world, laughter's the treat.
Curving conversations go on all day,
In a fruity way, come out and play!

In the Heart of the Orchard

In a grove where laughter grows,
The fruit seems to wear a nose.
Swinging high on branches sway,
Telling jokes to pass the day.

Squirrels giggle as they glide,
While bees buzz with joy and pride.
A swing made from a yellow peel,
Is the happiest ride you'll feel.

Sunshine tickles all around,
Even shadows wear a crown.
A dance party starts with glee,
Every critter joins to see.

Under leaves of emerald green,
A whimsical world can be seen.
Each giggle echoes joy and cheer,
In this orchard, fun is near.

Floating in Bliss

Clouds are cushions in the sky,
Where silly thoughts begin to fly.
Gliding high with giggles bright,
Chasing dreams till the fall of night.

A boat made from a fruit so sweet,
Adventures travel with our feet.
Waves of laughter swell and crest,
In this journey, we're the guests.

Whispers of a breeze so bold,
Carrying stories yet untold.
A splash of color, bright and clear,
Every laugh rings far and near.

Floating on a bubble's pop,
We'll never want this ride to stop.
With every giggle, joy will grow,
In this wonder, let us flow.

Fables Beneath the Sun

Where the sun spills tales of cheer,
A monkey's grin brings smiles near.
Funny fables on tree limbs sway,
Tickling our thoughts as they play.

At noon, the shadows start to dance,
Every creature takes a chance.
A parrot squawks a silly tune,
While ants march in a comical croon.

The grass sings songs of silly things,
As laughter spreads on vibrant wings.
A giggly breeze joins in the fun,
Creating chaos under the sun.

With each tale spun so absurd,
Echoes of joy are heard.
We weave our stories, wild and free,
In this fable festivity.

Sipping on Sunshine

In a cup filled to the brim,
A swirl of bright, a happy whim.
With a straw that bends and loops,
We sip our giggles in joyful scoops.

The flavor is laughter, sweet and pure,
Each sip dances, we want more.
Sunshine fills our hearts with cheer,
Tickling our toes, drawing us near.

A party held in tiny sips,
Where every slurp brings funny quips.
Floating flavors, dreams align,
In this sunlight, we feel divine.

Each drop a sparkle, bright and bold,
Adventures in this drink we hold.
Together, let's toast to the fun,
Sipping joy till the day is done.

Sunshine Stories and Gleeful Whirls

Under the bright sun, we laugh and we play,
Chasing our shadows, not a care in the day.
With ice cream dripping and giggles so bold,
We dance on the grass, as the warmth takes hold.

The clouds wear smiles, they float in such glee,
Tickling the trees, as we sing with the bees.
A world made of giggles, a realm full of jest,
In this shining kingdom, we find our sweet rest.

Enchanted Trails of Laughter and Light.

On trails where the giggles twirl in the breeze,
We skip with our snacks, our hearts aim to please.
Each step brings a chuckle, each glance is a grin,
As laughter erupts, let the joy now begin.

With sparkles of sunshine, we bask and we roll,
Silly hats tilted, with a wink at our soul.
Chasing the rainbows that dance in the air,
In this whimsical world, we are free, without care.

Tropical Whispers

In a land where the coconuts giggle with glee,
The palm trees do sway, like they're wild and free.
With each little whisper, a joke starts to bloom,
We laugh till the stars sprinkle light in the room.

A breeze full of chuckles, a tide full of cheer,
We skip through the sand, letting worries disappear.
Bright colors exploding, like bursts of delight,
In this playful paradise, everything feels right.

Yellow Curves of Fantasy

Curved yellow treasures swing low on the vine,
Teasing the taste buds, a fruit so divine.
With laughter erupting, we gather in cheer,
The sweetness of moments we hold ever near.

In a world full of whims, colors twist and twirl,
Funny faces appear with each joyful whirl.
Our dreams take flight on the wings of a song,
In this zany adventure, together we belong.

Lush Thoughts in a Banana Grove

In a grove where the giggles grow,
The fruit wears a smile, nice and slow.
Monkeys dance, their tails all a-twirl,
Chasing sunbeams, oh, what a swirl.

With every peel, a chuckle slips,
Sticky fingers and fruity trips.
Laughter echoes through leafy lanes,
As joy pops like sweet candy canes.

Sunlight tricks through the tangled vines,
A playful breeze, each branch entwines.
Giggling leaves whisper silly jokes,
In this patch, the wildest pokes.

So let's all bounce in this funny field,
Where nature's secrets are laid revealed.
Winking fruits and antics bright,
In the grove, everything feels right.

Euphoria Wrapped in Nature's Bounty

Beneath the canopy, dreams take flight,
With treasures bright that feel just right.
Golden slips that shimmer and gleam,
Together we twirl, lost in a dream.

Juicy wonders at our fingertips,
We giggle and dance, no need for scripts.
Nature's bounty, oh what a thrill,
Tickling our hearts, giving a chill.

Silly squirrels swing from the trees,
Chasing delights in a warm summer breeze.
A chorus of chuckles fills the space,
With fruits that bring a playful grace.

All wrapped in joy, we tiptoe around,
Where laughter and harmony are found.
When nature offers such sweet reprieve,
The world feels light, it's hard to believe.

Sun-Kissed Shadows of Sunkissed Wishes

In corners where shadows play hide and seek,
Our wildest desires are bold and unique.
Peels that glisten in the golden rays,
Sparkling laughter brightens our days.

A shade of mischief drapes down low,
As we frolic in the sun's warm glow.
Each fruit is a canvas, splattered with cheer,
Where ordinary moments turn sublime here.

Imaginary feasts dance on the air,
With fruity fantasies beyond compare.
Whimsical giggles ripple wide,
As nature's charms turn the tide.

Wishes flutter like butterflies near,
Embracing silliness, we shed every fear.
In this bright haven of playful bliss,
Every sweet moment is one we won't miss.

Kaleidoscope of Serotonin and Sun

Twisting colors like a vivid dream,
Fruity flashes dance in a gleam.
Each chuckle bursts in iridescent plays,
As we savor laughter in a multitude of ways.

Twirling in hues of bright canary,
A jester's anthem, never contrary.
Golden giggles float in the air,
Whirling around without a care.

Mood swings with a wink and a nudge,
Nature's comedy has us in a grudge.
Slipping and sliding on this joyful ride,
A playful paradise we can't hide.

So raise a toast to this silly spree,
Where each bright moment sets us free.
Crafted with joy, in the world's embrace,
A kaleidoscope spin through this happy place.

Mirage of a Dreamy Orchard

In an orchard bright, with sunlight's beams,
Frogs wear hats, and dancers weave dreams.
With every twist, a giggle erupts,
As shadows prance, their shapes corrupts.

The trees they whisper, secrets they share,
Fruits play tag with the light summer air.
A banana split, on a swing set swings,
While squirrels plot to steal silly things.

Clouds giggle down, as they softly float,
Tickling branches, each leaf on a boat.
The air is thick with sweetened laughter,
As dreams take flight, chasing ever after.

Plums pretend to be pirates up high,
Berries argue on who gets the sky.
In this wacky, wild, vibrant spree,
Life's zany tune sings beautifully free.

Whimsical Sway

A dance in a field where the sun gives chase,
Chickens in tutus find their own grace.
Wiggly worms wear glittery shoes,
And giggle with glee at the latest news.

The breeze starts to hum a jovial tune,
While daffodils sway like a cartoon.
Each petal leaps, full of joyous pride,
In this quirky world, let's take a ride.

Snails on surfboards glide down the lanes,
While laughter erupts like soft, summer rains.
Butterflies giggle, painted in hues,
As the daisies tap shoes in vibrant views.

Time seems to drift with a wink and a nod,
With merry chaos that's gloriously flawed.
In the garden, oh what a game we play,
Living the upside-down, fun-filled ballet.

The Orbit of Delirium

In a cosmic swirl where the oddities spin,
Lemons juggle stars with a cheeky grin.
The moon rides a bike, with a grin on its face,
While comets collide in a dreamy embrace.

The planets wear shoes made of fluffy clouds,
Dancing to tunes from the silvery crowds.
Saturn's rings play hopscotch in line,
With giggles that echo through space, so divine.

Galaxies twirl in a whimsical race,
With meteors flying in a dizzying chase.
Laughter erupts in the void's vast dome,
As we drift through the silly, spectacular foam.

Stars toast to the fun, with milkshakes aglow,
Wishing on wishes, we'll never outgrow.
In this orbit of joy, there's never a fuss,
Just buoyant delights that enchant all of us.

Juicy Vignettes

Sliced sunshine dances in whimsical bowls,
Silly little critters have wonderful roles.
Kiwis are chatting, all vibrant and bright,
As apricots gossip under soft, gentle light.

Lemons play tic-tac-toe under trees,
While raspberries dash on a soft summer breeze.
Cherries giggle as they sway to and fro,
Counting their spots, as they trade tales low.

In this patchwork world, everything's gumdrops,
Morsels of laughter that never quite stops.
Hilarity bubbles in every sweet bite,
Crafting our stories from morning till night.

So slice up the whimsy, bring joy to the feast,
In flavors combined, we savor every least.
These juicy adventures are seldom so tame,
As life in the orchard embraces the game.

Golden Curves of Whimsy

In the garden, giggles grow,
With golden curves, a silly show.
Fragrant breezes tickle the air,
Bouncing fruits dance without a care.

Silly hats on leafy heads,
Whirling colors, mischief spreads.
Splashing puddles, joy releases,
In this world, all laughter increases.

Snickering squirrels join the fray,
Chasing shadows, bright and cray.
Beneath the trees, we all convene,
To play in nature's vibrant scene.

Whimsical thoughts take flight today,
With quirks and giggles on display.
We'll share a smile beneath the skies,
In a world where whimsy never dies.

Dappled Sunlight and Sweet Delusions

In the patch where sunlight beams,
Lies a land of giggling dreams.
Sweet illusions frolic near,
Chasing shadows, full of cheer.

Round the bend, the laughter swells,
Echoing through dappled shells.
Frolicking pets, with tails so bright,
Join the fun in pure delight.

Whispers of mirth paint the air,
As rabbits juggle, unaware.
Tickled by the sun's warm rays,
Dance and play through silly days.

Each giggle, a note in a song,
In this place, we all belong.
So raise a cheer, forget your gloom,
In the garden of sweet perfume.

Yellow Silhouettes in the Mind

Flashes of yellow flash about,
It's a merry-go-round, no doubt.
Bright shapes wiggle, twist, and spin,
With each chuckle, they pull you in.

Imagined critters dance away,
With silly hats, they love to play.
Wisps of laughter swirl around,
While goofy moments know no bounds.

Snapshots of joy fill the air,
Dancing shadows everywhere.
In this playful, sunny frame,
Nothing here is ever the same.

Sketches of whimsy softly glow,
As laughter leads the way, you know.
Beneath bright skies, we swing and sway,
With warmth that lingers throughout the day.

Dreams of Tropical Reverie

In a realm of fruity delight,
Squirrels plan by day and night.
Juggling treats upon their head,
They laugh and dance, never dread.

Coconut waves wash on the shore,
Where giggles echo evermore.
The sunshine sparks a playful wink,
As merriment flows like a drink.

Crickets chirp in playful tune,
Beneath the smiling silver moon.
Tropical breezes, sweet and light,
Carry laughter far and bright.

So grab a friend and leap with glee,
In this land of harmony.
With every chuckle, sung with pride,
Together we'll take the playful ride.

Dreams in a Fruit Bowl

In the fruit bowl where giggles hide,
Lemons wear hats, and apples slide.
Pineapples sway, feeling quite grand,
While cherries dance hand in hand.

Mangoes tell tales of sweet summer bliss,
As oranges laugh, thinking of this.
Grapes form a band, all dressed in green,
Playing tunes that are silly and keen.

A banana rolled out for its big show,
Slipped on a peel, oh what a flow!
The fruit bowl erupted in fits of cheer,
As fruits made mischief, spreading good cheer.

So when you find fruit in a bowl so bright,
Remember the laughter, the sheer delight.
For in each juicy morsel, you'll see,
A world full of joy, and a pinch of glee.

Sunlit Reverie

Under the sun where the laughter flies,
Lemonade rivers meet cotton candy skies.
A sweet little squirrel in a tiny hat,
Guards cupcake castles where dreams go splat.

Worms in bow ties crawl at a pace,
Dressed for a gala in a funny race.
Hopping and bouncing, they jive right along,
Singing the chatter of the fruit fly's song.

Coconut clouds burst with a giggling sound,
While fruit tart bushes dance all around.
The sun winks down, a playful glance,
As shadows skip by in a bumbling dance.

In a world of sweetness, come take a glance,
Every moment invites you to dance.
With giggles and glee, let the fun unfold,
In a sunlit land where dreams are bold.

Chasing Sunbeams

Around the yard where the daisies bloom,
A whirlwind of giggles bursts like a fume.
Butterflies pirouette in joyful flight,
As ladybugs giggle under the light.

A bouncing bubble floats past my nose,
Carrying secrets that nobody knows.
It pops with a sprinkle of glittery cheer,
Sparking a dance that draws everyone near.

Twirling and swirling, the beams start to play,
In the happy kingdom where clouds drift away.
Whiskers of kittens peek out from their spree,
Among peonies bright, it's a whimsical spree.

So chase the sunbeams that lead to delight,
With laughter and games that last through the night.
In fields of wonder, let your heart roam,
For in chasing the light, you will find your home.

A Slice of Serendipity

Imagine a slice of the sweetest bliss,
A sprinkle of laughter, a buttery kiss.
Cookies dance wildly atop the warm stove,
While pickles debate their odd little grove.

A sandwich stands proud, its layers amazed,
While mustard and ketchup engage in a craze.
Potato chips giggle, all crisp and bright,
In culinary antics that spark pure delight.

The dazzled fruit salad sings out a tune,
Beneath the joy of a bright harvest moon.
Every morsel a canvas of laughter and cheer,
Creating a masterpiece year after year.

So dig into life, where the flavors combine,
With a side of hilarity right down the line.
In the banquet of moments, let each day flip,
For a slice of serendipity's a sweet little trip.

The Joyful Echoes of Nature's Lullaby

In a patch of sun, a couple of gnomes,
Dance with the shadows, far from their homes.
Whispers of laughter, tickling the air,
Chasing away worries, no one a care.

Socks on their heads, what a comical sight,
Twirling through grass, sheer pure delight.
The flowers all giggle as they sway and bow,
Nature's own jesters, they're laughing somehow.

Fluffy clouds tap dance, on the warm summer sky,
While ants in tuxedos march by oh so spry.
Melodies of merriment float on the breeze,
Inviting us all for a life full of ease.

Echoes of joy, in each rustling leaf,
A symphony forging, beyond our belief.
With every soft chuckle, the world feels renewed,
In this grand orchestra, happiness brewed.

Flights of Fancy in a Garden of Gold

Butterflies flit with a wink and a grin,
In golden-hued blooms, let the fun begin.
Picnics with giggles, laughter on plates,
Jelly bean skies where the sweet creature waits.

Worms in top hats, they dance 'round the soil,
While daisies conspire, making mischief so loyal.
Their petals pirouette, what a splendid show,
Underneath the sun's warm, delightful glow.

Bunnies in bow ties share secrets and tales,
While slips of fresh breeze tickle their trails.
Chasing their shadows in high-flying loops,
Each patch of green filled with whimsical troops.

A fountain of giggles springs up from the ground,
With each joyful splash, more joy is found.
Under the chatter of chirpy delight,
A dance of pure whimsy lasts deep into night.

Bouncing Thoughts on Soft Breezes

Thoughts like rubber balls, they bounce all around,
Silly ideas spring forth, hop on the ground.
A frog in a top hat sells tickets to a show,
Where jellybeans jive in a marzipan flow.

Bubbles float by, whispering dreams with a grin,
As marshmallow clouds let the laughter pour in.
Frisbees of sunshine soar past with a cheer,
Filling the sky with a tickle of clear.

Kites made from laughter are ready to soar,
Dancing with delight from shore to the shore.
Each wobbly giggle, a ball of pure glee,
Reflects in the puddles, as bright as can be.

As moonlight spills secrets on fields of delight,
Thoughts bounce even faster, in the soft night light.
With fairies and frogs leading the grand parade,
Every jump feels like magic, never to fade.

Citrus Melodies of the Heart

In a grove of delights, where oranges can sing,
Lemons laugh lightly, sharing a fling.
Each slice tells a joke as the juiciest fruit,
Bouncing from branches, they dance in their suit.

Wiggly worms waddle in a tango of zest,
With cheerful green leaves, giving life their best.
Peppy little critters all sway to the beat,
In this citrus parade, who can resist the sweet?

Limes tap their toes, shaking zestful cheer,
While grapefruit giggles and winks with good cheer.
A melody ripples through branches and sun,
As fragrant delights have their joyful fun.

In breezy ballads, joy bubbles and twirls,
Where fruits really know how to toss and to hurl.
Each note is a laugh, sweet and bright like a start,
Singing in harmony, straight from the heart.

Feast of the Imagination

In a land where giggles grow,
A feast of nonsense on the go.
Frogs wear hats, and cats can sing,
Oh, what joy such dreams can bring.

Plates of jelly, skies of pie,
Dancing cakes that float up high.
Grapes in tutus, they parade,
In this world, no plans are made.

Clouds of candy drift and sway,
Lollipops chase the clouds away.
A river made of fizzy drink,
Let's grab a glass and have a wink.

With tickles sprinkled everywhere,
Life's a joke, we breathe the air.
Join the fun and take a seat,
In this madcap life so sweet!

Colorful Wandering Spirits

Whimsical whispers in the breeze,
We follow them with giggles and ease.
Trees that giggle, flowers that sway,
Join the dance of this bright play.

Bouncing balls of fluff and cheer,
Fuzzy friends from far and near.
Colorful spirits laughing loud,
In their company, we feel proud.

Chasing shadows, making friends,
Every corner, magic bends.
Silly sounds and joyful words,
Lifting hearts like tiny birds.

With every skip, we twirl and spin,
Where the fun never seems to end.
In this world of happy quirks,
Life's a treasure full of perks!

Journey Through the Orchard

In a land where fruit can laugh,
Adventure starts with a funny giraffe.
He wears a tie made out of leaves,
And shares the joy, with all who believe.

Apples rolling down the hill,
Chased by laughter, oh what a thrill!
Plump peaches giggle, run, and play,
In this quirky, sunlit sway.

Bouncing berries sing a tune,
Underneath the shining moon.
Every step, a joke unfolds,
In this orchard, laughter molds.

Join the prance, don't be shy,
Let's explore the zany sky!
Where fruit and fun forever blend,
And every moment is a friend.

Floating Fragments of Joy

Tiny bubbles in the air,
Popping giggles everywhere.
Jellybeans dancing in the breeze,
A silly life, if you please!

Feathers drift and tickle toes,
Merry mischief, who really knows?
Skipping stones that laugh and chat,
In this world, no room for flat.

Wobbly clouds with silly hats,
Whisper secrets like the bats.
They chuckle softly as we float,
On frothy waves of a dreamy boat.

Embrace the whimsy, let it sway,
A world where silliness holds sway.
With every laugh, a sparkle bright,
In fragments of joy, we take flight!

Dreamy Echoes in the Orchard

In a grove where shadows play,
A yellow fruit takes flight today.
It giggles as it swings so free,
Chasing clouds like bumblebees.

Laughter rises with the breeze,
Whispers swirl through tangled trees.
Silly thoughts like bubbles pop,
Making all the worries stop.

A frolicsome parade begins,
With fruits adorned in cheerful grins.
Twirling 'round in misty light,
Dancing 'til the fall of night.

In this orchard, no one's sour,
Each moment blossoms like a flower.
With every chuckle, joy expands,
As dreams take flight in golden strands.

Sunlit Fancies

Under sunbeams, smiles abound,
A fruity feast for all we've found.
Jokes are shared with every bite,
As giggles twinkle, pure delight.

Sipping sunshine from our cups,
Slipping on our garden flips.
Each tasty treat a playful jest,
Tickling senses, such a quest!

With laughter echoing through the air,
We toss the peels without a care.
Fanciful ideas whirl like fish,
In this feast, we find our bliss.

So come and join this merry spree,
Where mirth and sweetness roam so free.
In the warmth of laughter's glow,
We scatter joy like petals blow.

The Allure of Whimsy

A crooked smile, a sunny giggle,
Strolling trees that sway and wiggle.
Banana boats on rivers wide,
Sailing dreams on giggling tide.

Jumpy jests in every bite,
Swinging low beneath the light.
With every tumble, more surprise,
As silly thoughts dance in our eyes.

Chasing echoes, leaps and bounds,
Clutching treasures that surround.
Hands reach up to touch the breeze,
As laughter floats among the leaves.

In this land of vibrant cheer,
Whimsy draws us ever near.
Join the fun where smiles gleam,
In the heart of every dream.

Glimpses of Summer Solstice

Underneath a bubble sky,
Where fruity fantasies float by.
We tip our hats to wayward glee,
Where sunshine dances wild and free.

Soft whispers drift on every breeze,
As laughter's light it teases trees.
Sugar-coated with hints of cheer,
The joyous songs we long to hear.

In this moment, time stands still,
With every sweet and sassy thrill.
Hand in hand, we chase the sun,
Looking for the silliest fun.

As dusk begins to paint the sky,
We twirl and jump, no need to shy.
With every chuckle, spirits rise,
In the warmth of twilight's sigh.

www.ingramcontent.com/pod-product-compliance
Lightning Source LLC
Chambersburg PA
CBHW060113230426
43661CB00003B/173